Feodor Dostoevsky

By ERNEST J. SIMMONS

 *Columbia University Press*
NEW YORK & LONDON 1969

COLUMBIA ESSAYS ON MODERN WRITERS is a series of critical studies of English, Continental, and other writers whose works are of contemporary artistic and intellectual significance.

Editor: William York Tindall

Advisory Editors
Jacques Barzun   W. T. H. Jackson   Joseph A. Mazzeo

Feodor Dostoevsky is Number 40 of the series

ERNEST J. SIMMONS was formerly Professor of Russian Literature at Columbia University. Among his books are *Leo Tolstoy, Dostoevski: The Making of a Novelist, Chekhov,* and *Introduction to Russian Realism.*

Copyright © 1969 Columbia University Press
Library of Congress Catalog Card Number: 77–76252
Printed in the United States of America

Feodor Dostoevsky

One is now surprised when a Soviet literary critic writes: "A great advance in our knowledge of thinking and creativity is needed to understand why, for example, Albert Einstein believed that he had obtained more from Dostoevsky than from Carl Friedrich Gauss, one of the greatest physicists, astronomers, and mathematicians." For, years ago, Lenin, when asked what he thought about Dostoevsky's novels, is reported to have replied: "I have no time for such trash." And though Gorky extolled Dostoevsky's genius and compared him to Shakespeare, he condemned him as a "petty-bourgeois and defeatist," guilty of the unpardonable sin in Soviet morality of selfish individualism, which is as certain, Gorky concluded, "as there are no goats without a smell." And the anti-Soviet Vladimir Nabokov, who is partial to the dissidence of dissent in things literary, not unexpectedly lines up on Lenin's side of the barricades when he asserts that Dostoevsky is "a much overrated sentimental and Gothic novelist of the time . . . one of those megaphones of elephantine platitudes."

Nevertheless, there has never been any question of Dostoevsky's position as a novelist and thinker among his countrymen. A staggering bibliography about every phase of his life and work has accumulated. Even Soviet critics, though they regard him as a political reactionary, an admirer of tsars, and a professed believer in Russian Orthodoxy, are not disposed to leave him safe and undisturbed in his prerevolutionary immortality, for he is one of the most widely read of the great nineteenth-century Russian novelists and has exercised a profound influ-

[3]

ence on some of the best Soviet writers. The wealth of Soviet critical and scholarly literature on Dostoevsky is of primary importance for our understanding of him.

Some evidence supports the notion that the upsurge of Dostoevsky's popularity in the Soviet Union since Stalin's death is simply another manifestation—in reverse so to speak— of a renewal of the historical trend of Russian "Westernization" in cultural as well as in social and economic endeavors. For between the two World Wars and afterwards no nineteenth-century novelist has received as much attention in Western Europe and the United States as Dostoevsky, although critical appraisal has tended to concentrate upon his significance as a prophet, philosopher, psychologist, and as a political, social, and religious thinker rather than as a literary artist. All this is perhaps understandable in our own day of hard choices in intellectual loyalties, for many political, moral, and religious problems that have disturbed generations during these years were most effectively dramatized in Dostoevsky's celebrated works.

The doctrine of Nietzsche, who admitted indebtedness to Dostoevsky's psychology, that the creator of good or evil must first destroy all values resembles closely that of Shigalev in *The Possessed*. And by the time Thomas Masaryk's *Spirit of Russia* appeared in 1913, which singled out Dostoevsky as the key figure in the development of Russian nineteenth-century thought, a veritable cult of Dostoevsky had begun to sweep over the intellectual world of Western Europe. Before the advent of Hitler, one German critic went so far as to say that since Luther's time there had been no greater spiritual influence on Germany than Dostoevsky. Later Malraux testified that Dostoevsky had profoundly affected the whole intellectual history of his generation in France. Indeed, Sartre has paid tribute to Dostoevsky whose condemnation of the tyranny of reason provided inspiration for the existentialist belief that human action becomes simply the expression of a biological urge to self-assertion. And Camus also, in *L'Homme révolté*, drew heavily upon the agonizing questions propounded in *The Brothers Karamazov* in elaborating his thesis that the mistaken belief in reason in modern times has led to a loss of all sense of values and to the cynical seizure of power by dictators.

By the time it reached the United States this European cult had somewhat dwindled, but during the last twenty years American interest in Dostoevsky has been on a rising scale. If the test of a great writer is not so much what he says but what he does to us—the extent to which he imposes his vision and transforms our own experience—then in these terms Dostoevsky seems to make a special appeal today to American readers. Though the focus of our interest does not exclude aesthetic considerations, it is mainly concerned with social, political, and religious problems involved in the throbbing human dramas of his characters and with his extraordinary psychological probing of their tormented lives. It is also possible that we feel a special kinship with the "sick consciousness" of these troubled men and women as they struggle to realize their identity in a world from which they are alienated. For Dostoevsky's anti-heroes, like those in so much contemporary American fiction, are overwhelmed with the infirmity of doubt, caught in the treadmill of endless reflection, and doomed to inertia because of a lack of will.

Unlike his great contemporaries Turgenev and Tolstoy, members of wealthy, cultured families of the landed gentry, Dostoevsky (born 1821) belonged to a family perched insecurely on the lower rung of the Moscow middle-class ladder—he called himself an "intellectual proletarian." The family had no pretensions to culture, and his father, an ex-army surgeon, harsh and rigid in domestic matters, was subsequently murdered by serfs on the small property he owned in the country. This disparity in social position and educational training influenced Dostoevsky's literary interests and the subjects of his novels, so different from those of Turgenev and Tolstoy.

At the age of seventeen Dostoevsky entered the St. Petersburg Military Engineering School, and during five years there he devoted all the spare time he could steal from dull drill and the science of fortifications to reading belles-lettres. A high degree of intellectual curiosity was part of his intense nature. Besides Russian authors, of whom his favorites were Pushkin and Gogol, he read a variety of foreign writers: Homer, Shakespeare, Corneille, Racine, Rousseau, Goethe, Byron, and Schiller, the last with an enthusiasm he never lost (Schiller and the Schlegels contributed much to his later aesthetic theorizing). His youthful delight in stories of adventure was fed by Gothic romances of Ann Radcliffe, "Monk" Lewis, Maturin, and E. T. A. Hoffmann, translations of which had a vogue in Russia at that time. Their lurid trappings and scenes no doubt encouraged his taste for the melodramatic and for plots of violence and crime which later entered into the structure of his own fiction. Nor did he neglect novelists who could lay claims to realism, such as Walter Scott, Balzac, Hugo, George Sand, and Eugène Sue.

Not much information exists about Dostoevsky's developing personality during these formative years, but there is evidence enough to suggest that the shy, secretive, lonely image portrayed in biographies is somewhat at variance with the facts. He could be all these things when thrust into contact with official bureaucrats or social superiors, but he also enjoyed nights out with fellow-cadets, good food and drink, interesting conversation, music, theater, and the company of girls. There was a plunging, all-or-nothing quality in his nature that manifested itself in early gambling bouts and grandiose plans for achieving quick financial successes, although he was nearly always improvident in money matters. It was a time for dreaming and he was a passionate dreamer about fame, self-sacrificing deeds, and idealistic friendships.

By 1843 when Dostoevsky had finished his professional training, the career of army engineer had given way to the determination to write. He felt that he had something to say in literature and had already begun his apprenticeship by translating Balzac's *Eugénie Grandet*. In the fall of the next year he wrote his brother Mikhail: "Here is my hope. I am finishing a novel of the size of *Eugénie Grandet*. The novel is rather original." At the age of twenty-three he resigned his commission in the service, revised and recopied his novel again and again, and in the spring of 1845, with many misgivings and entirely unsure of his talent, allowed a young friend to take the finished manuscript of *Poor Folk* to the leading literary critic Vissarion Belinsky for his judgment. Many years later, in *The Diary of a Writer*, Dostoevsky recalled with deep feeling Belinsky's ecstatic reaction. He extolled the infallible artistic instinct with which Dostoevsky had revealed the hidden nature of his hero. "That is the secret of high artistic value," Belinsky declared, "That is truth in art! That is the artist's service to truth! The truth has been revealed and announced to you as an artist, it has been brought as a gift; value this gift and remain faithful to it, and you will be a great writer!"

Though the short novel *Poor Folk* (1846) has some of the usual faults of the beginner, Belinsky's lofty praise was prophetically correct, for he realized that Dostoevsky had created something quite new in Russian fiction. This story of an impoverished, elderly copying clerk who struggles hopelessly for respectability and conceals his real love for a poor orphaned girl beneath a sentimentally expressed paternal affection was the first Russian social novel. This fact and the story's implied condemnation of society's unconcern for the underprivileged delighted the liberal reformer Belinsky and won enthusiastic response from readers. Pushkin's rather exceptional short story of lowly people, "The Station Master" (1830), and Gogol's famous "The Overcoat" (1842)—one of Gogol's works that had persuaded Belinsky to acclaim him as the founder of the "natural school"— certainly helped to inspire *Poor Folk* and led the critic to regard Dostoevsky as a disciple of the "natural school." Dostoevsky had discovered the fantastic reality of the city's humiliated and injured and he became their poet. In part he introduced to Russia the emphasis of the humanitarian literature of the West which at this time was supplanting socially privileged heroes and heroines with those from the poor and rejected, as in the novels of George Sand, Eugène Sue, and Dickens. And the epistolary form of his first novel was prompted not so much by Richardson's *Clarissa* or Rousseau's *Nouvelle Héloïse* as by George Sand's *Jacques* whose hero has been compared with Devushkin in *Poor Folk*.

But unlike Gogol or any possible predecessors in this vein of writing, Dostoevsky added a new dimension—an intense psychological interest in which the conflict of his hero is not observed from the outside but is profoundly analyzed from within. Belinsky and others, he wrote his brother about *Poor Folk*, "find in me a new and original spirit in that I proceed by analysis and not by synthesis, that is, I plunge into the depths, and, while analyzing every atom, I search out the whole." The result was a piercing insight into the tragic futility of poor people in love, people victimized by cruel circumstances of contemporary society. Dostoevsky's handling of the ensuing psychological drama established the fact that with *Poor Folk* he had begun his own school of Russian realistic fiction.

With literary success came social success and both went to the head of the youthful Dostoevsky. Bumptiously he wrote his brother of endless invitations to salons and dinners by well-bred nobles and literary celebrities. But this short, fair-haired man, with small gray eyes, sickly complexion, and nervously twitching lips, cut a sorry figure in polished society. He was awkward in his movements, ill at ease, and in conversation alternated between prolonged silences and fiery monologues. Extremely sensitive, he soon realized that he was out of place in such a milieu.

Fortunately Dostoevsky's mind was on writing and he quickly followed up his first effort with another short novel, *The Double* (1846). More confident now of his powers, he announced to his brother that the new tale was "ten times superior to *Poor Folk*. Our crowd says that since *Dead Souls* there has never been anything like it in Russia, that the work is one of genius, and what do they not say!" Despite the laughable comparison to a full-length novel and a great masterpiece, Dostoevsky, like Gogol, had striven for originality but in a much more limited sphere of narrative art. *The Double* is an amazing study (for its time) in abnormal psychology. The hero, Golyadkin, a minor civil servant, afflicted by a growing persecution mania, encounters a man who looks exactly like him and bears the same name. At first Golyadkin befriends him and secures a position for him in his office. The remainder of the story relates in meticulous detail the hero's adventures with his Double. With mounting indignation Golyadkin observes him winning the praise and favor of his superiors and fellow-workers which he himself had tried so vainly to achieve. In his deranged mind the Double becomes the leader of a conspiracy against him and he makes futile efforts to denounce the insolent fellow. After a final series of events in which his rival humiliates him, the tale ends with the Double helping Golyadkin into a carriage on his way to an insane asylum.

The ability with which Dostoevsky sustains the illusion of the Double and the subtleness of his psychological insight into Golyadkin's warped mind reveal the young author's impressive artistic skill. The hero's mental disorder is not unrelated to a form of spiritual illness induced by social factors that oppress him. This first attempt at analyzing a split personality seems to be connected with Dostoevsky's later preoccupation with various aspects of dualism in the creation of some of his most memorable characters. Though he never again pushes the pathological aspects quite so far as in the case of Golyadkin, he comes close to it in the famous scene in *The Brothers Karamazov* where Ivan is confronted by his Double who so effectively exposes his ambivalence.

Belinsky praised *The Double* when he first heard parts of it in manuscript, but his enthusiasm waned after he read it in print—he found the story incompatible with the social significance he demanded in literature. Worse still the public pronounced it boring. In a spirit of self-criticism that contrasts admirably with his previous self-praise, Dostoevsky wrote his brother of the failure of *The Double* and then added: "I have a terrible vice: unlimited pride and ambition. The idea that I deceived expectations and spoiled something that could have been a great story has crushed me." Many years later he admitted in *The Diary of a Writer* that the form of the tale had been entirely unsuccessful, but, he insisted: "I never projected a more serious idea in literature."

Between the remainder of 1846 and 1849, when Dostoevsky's early literary period was brought to an abrupt end by his arrest, he wrote more short stories and sketches, such as "Mr. Prokharchin," "The Landlady," "A Faint Heart," and "The Honest Thief." And shortly after *Poor Folk* appeared he had also embarked upon his first full-length novel. He obviously intended it to be a major work and an answer to Belinsky and his followers who by now had dismissed him as a failure. Planned as a psychological novel in depth, *Netochka Nezvanova* began to appear in *Fatherland Notes* in 1849. But only three episodes, the third unfinished, had been published when Dostoevsky's arrest put an end to the work. He never resumed it, perhaps because he recognized its lack of compositional and stylistic unity.

Each of the episodes is in the form of a separate tale connected by the continuing presence of the narrator Netochka, a pattern that may have been inspired by Lermontov's *Hero of Our Time*. In the first Netochka tells of her childhood with her mother and stepfather, Yefimov, whose talent as a violinist is frustrated by his self-abuse, a confession of defeat that seems to reflect Dostoevsky's own artistic self-disparagement at this time. The little girl is brilliantly drawn. One is impressed by Dostoevsky's technique in the difficult matter of child psychology, employed so effectively in the later novels, especially in his treatment of Netochka's morbid love for her wayward stepfather and her guilt over her dislike for her mother. The second episode is concerned with Netochka's adoption, after the death of her parents, into a wealthy family and her passionate love affair there with Katya, the young daughter of the household. The marked contrast between the meek Netochka and proud Katya in their love-hate relationship anticipates similar contrasts in characterizations in the great novels. In the unfinished third episode the only notable creation is the sinister vengeful husband of Netochka's benefactress who gives evidence of developing into a towering figure of wickedness. This unfinished novel, which Dostoevsky reprinted in his collected works in revised form, is noteworthy as an indication of rapidly maturing art and as offering a kind of preview of ideas, images, characterizations, and devices, such as the philosophical dialogue or monologue, that would repeatedly appear in novels to come.

In a fugitive sense one may perceive the main direction of Dostoevsky's future creative development in the writing of this first literary period. Some characters are preliminary studies of later more famous ones. They are dreamy, unpractical people or wretched clerks and poor students who live in unsavory corners of St. Petersburg. Though they are not entirely creatures born of literary influences, neither are they in every respect the result of a young man's limited observations of life around him. His intense analysis of their feelings, however, reflects his own emotional, spiritual, and psychological self-examination. But an experience was awaiting him that would deepen his perception of human nature and develop his genius for revealing the inner struggle that goes on in the souls of suffering men and women.

Opposing views on art were the real reason for Dostoevsky's break with Belinsky. The famous critic's social and political beliefs led him to reject "pure art." His approach was a utilitarian one: literature must reveal the life of the masses and in analyzing the contemporary human condition must pass judgment on it. Dostoevsky's position at this time contained elements of an idealistic Kantian aesthetic; it stressed "pure form," the free play of the mind, art without a purpose. He emphasized the autonomy of art and the irrationality of the creative act, in which ideas, problems, questions, theories, dreams, and hypotheses lead to mental struggle and intellectual drama out of which emerges an artistically realistic vision of life. On the other hand, Dostoevsky, who was a firm believer in autocracy and the Russian Orthodox faith, was powerfully affected by Belinsky's advocacy of socialism and atheism which he aimed against a reactionary church and the oppressive rule of Nicholas I.

It is not surprising, then, that Dostoevsky, seeking new friends after his rupture with Belinsky and his disciples, should have found them among the Friday gatherings at the home of the idealistic Mikhail Petrashevsky where discussions were held on writings of the French utopian socialists, Fourier, St. Simon, and Proudhon, and on the need for social reforms in Russia. But he also associated himself with a smaller group of more venture-some souls in these gatherings, the so-called Durov Circle, whose members, convinced that reforms could not be achieved by peaceful methods, secretly conspired to promote revolution-ary action to free the serfs. They planned to propagandize their views by printing their own writings on a clandestinely pro-cured hand press. It is also known that Dostoevsky repeatedly and enthusiastically read to members of both circles Belinsky's famous contraband letter to Gogol, in which, among other things, he excoriated the church and praised atheism.

The tsar's government, aware of these developments through police informers, and fearful of contagion from the revolution-ary turmoil in the West at this time, arrested members of the Petrashevsky Circle in April, 1849. After a long investigation, twenty-one prisoners, including Dostoevsky, were condemned to be shot. The memory of the horrible experience he and his comrades underwent during the grisly preparations for execu-tion that cold December morning in Semyonev Square before the tsar's commutation was announced haunted the pages of Dostoevsky's fiction. His sentence was changed to four years at hard labor in a prison at Omsk, Siberia, and thereafter four years as a soldier in the ranks.

It is important to realize, in the light of Dostoevsky's reaction to this catastrophe, that he had been involved in an illegal activity, and he drew upon the experience in writing *The Possessed* in the 1870s, a novel inspired by a political murder committed by the revolutionary S. G. Nechaev and his fellow-conspirators. "Probably I could never have become a *Nechaev*," he wrote in *The Diary of a Writer*, "but a follower of Nechaev, I am not certain; it may be I could have . . . in the days of my youth." In short, he believed his severe penalty justified, and like the sinning characters who achieve salvation by suffering in his future novels, he willingly accepted punishment as an atonement for his crime.

Dostoevsky served his sentence like any of the common murderers and thieves among whom he lived in chains, stench, and hard labor. He endured profound spiritual agony during the ordeal, and he dates his first epileptic seizures from this time. Eventually he got to know well many of his rough fellow-convicts and to admire them—"in one way or another, the most gifted of our people," he remarked. Though he was forbidden to write, his imagination actively worked on literary plans. "How many native types, characters, did I take with me from prison!" he later told his brother. "How many tales of vagabonds, robbers, and, in general, of the whole gloomy, wretched existence. There is enough for entire volumes. What a wonderful people! On the whole, I did not lose my time. If not Russia, then I have come to know the Russian people well, as well as only few knew them."

The New Testament was the only book allowed him in prison, and as though repenting for having embraced Belinsky's atheistic belief, he read it at every opportunity. He rediscovered Christ and found spiritual sustenance in the Gospels. Only Christ could raise up the sinner, comfort the fallen, and promise the humble of heart new life on earth. This faith brought him a serenity and assuaged the bitterness of prison existence. Not long after his release he wrote a woman, who had befriended him during this period, of his religious change: "Here it is: to believe that there is nothing more beautiful, more profound, more sympathetic, more reasonable, more manly, and more perfect than Christ, and not only is there nothing, but, I tell myself with jealous love, there can be nothing. Besides, if anyone proved to me that Christ was outside the truth, and it *really* was so that the truth was outside Christ, then I would prefer to remain with Christ than with the truth."

The statement is important, for unbelief is implicit in his very assertion of belief. The remainder of his life was to be a holy pilgrimage, an endless search for God, but he combined in his heart the most ardent faith with the greatest disbelief. Perhaps the search itself was the end, the spiritual bread of his existence and, one may add, of his artistic powers.

Dostoevsky entered prison a young radical and unbeliever, and he left it with a heightened respect for the authority of the crown and a new faith in the teachings of Christ. His experience had taught him the doctrine of salvation by suffering, and the New Testament had fortified his belief in it. Finally, he had discovered the virtues of the common Russian people and had become convinced of their special significance in the future fate of his country. In the growth of his creative art prison played not a negative but a positive role. It did not change his creative process; there was no essential break with the past in this respect. Prison defined and deepened his creative powers and provided him with rich material for the further study of the suffering individuals in whom he had been interested from the beginning. In his early works he had been concerned with the souls of the insulted and injured; in prison he learned to understand and to analyze them more profoundly than ever.

The chains were struck off Dostoevsky's ankles January 23, 1854, and upon release from prison he was ordered to Semipalatinsk, a Siberian garrison town, to serve as a common soldier. In keeping with the attitude of patient acceptance he had practiced in prison, he wrote his brother: "I do not complain; this is my cross and I have deserved it." He worked hard as a soldier and strove to win the approbation of his superiors. Starved for reading matter after four years of deprivation, he eagerly absorbed in his spare time quantities of books and magazines he requested from his brother. And once again he began to get the feel of the pen.

This uneventful existence was suddenly interrupted by his passionate love for a frail, sickly blonde, Marya Isaeva. She was married to a hopeless drunkard whose opportune death hardly improved Dostoevsky's situation—a young schoolteacher promptly claimed her favors. Life seemed to imitate art, for there is nothing more fantastic in Dostoevsky's fiction than this triangular love affair in which he went to unbelievable extremes to promote the cause of his rival while protesting his undying love for this rather pretty, flighty, and somewhat hysterical woman. (The deceased drunkard of a husband and Marya reappear as Marmeladov and his spouse in *Crime and Punishment*.) She married Dostoevsky in 1857, an alliance that turned out to be anything but happy.

Marriage increased his ever-present financial needs which now intensified the desire to write. As an ex-convict he required permission to publish, but he felt this would soon come for he had been promoted to a junior officer's rating. Various literary designs crowded his brain, ideas that he had thought out in prison. Yet he feared to spoil the major work he had in mind by beginning it prematurely; the conception of the central character, he decided, would take several years to mature in his imagination. Accordingly, the first two pieces he finished after release from prison have no connection with his experience there.

The long short story "Uncle's Dream" (1859) is one of Dostoevsky's best-wrought tales, a Gogolian satire on the sniveling society of a small provincial town for which Semipalatinsk must have been the model. At times situational humor leavens the exposure of cynical human foibles. The ancient prince, whom the town's dowager schemes to marry off to her daughter Zina, is a delightful caricature. The brilliant concluding scene, where the mother's deception is revealed to assembled townsfolk when the befuddled prince insists that his engagement to Zina is simply a beautiful dream, bears comparison with Gogol's famous concluding scene in his play *The Government Inspector*.

The humorous and tragic combine in the short novel *The Village of Stepanchikovo and Its Inhabitants* (1859), better known in English by the title *The Friend of the Family*. Dostoevsky thought this longer work "incomparably above" "Uncle's Dream," and at first he was most enthusiastic over its two main characters, Colonel Rostanev and Foma Opiskin, whom he described as "tremendously typical" and "faultlessly fashioned." Though the work continued the line of his early artistic development, it also opened up new perspectives of greater things to come. Rostanev's mother, a general's widow, arrives to settle on her son's estate, and after her appears Opiskin, a companion of her husband who had been degraded by him to the position of a family buffoon. Now, in altered circumstances, this vain, scheming, Russian Tartuffe, who aspired to be an author, gains an extraordinary ascendancy over the whole household, and especially over its meek master, Rostanev. Opiskin's ambitious effort is a palpable compensation for his former degradation. Dostoevsky concentrates on the psychological portrayal of this complex, dualistic creature, and the strength of the characterization saves the novel from being a mediocre work. The analytical treatment of Opiskin goes

[17]

beyond that of the ambivalent creations of the early tales. For now Dostoevsky suggests, in the conflict between self-esteem and self-abasement, a kind of reciprocity that is almost psychic; the two states of mind aid and abet each other. The dominant aspect of Opiskin's dualism—the desire to suffer and make others suffer—Dostoevsky developed more cogently in later characters. Critics have pointed out, and with some justification, that the frustrated author Opiskin is a parody of Gogol in that writer's more lamentable guise as a misdirected preacher of asceticism, moral nonsense, and futile religiosity.

Dostoevsky's hope that these two works, particularly *The Friend of the Family*, would help to revive the literary reputation he enjoyed before prison turned out to be disappointing— they went entirely unnoticed. More than ever he felt it necessary to get back to St. Petersburg among remembered scenes and friends who might encourage his writing. He obtained the aid of highly placed officials and wrote pleading letters and laudatory poems to members of the royal family. These expressions of patriotic sentiments and contrition for past offenses, however seemingly sycophantic, actually represented changed convictions since his prison experience. He was finally permitted to resign from the army and to settle in Tver. After some months of languishing there, a plea to the emperor that he required medical aid succeeded. Just ten years after he set out for Siberia in chains, he returned, in December, 1859, to his beloved St. Petersburg, a free man.

Life took on exquisite meaning again. Revolutionary elements in the capital wanted to glorify him as a former political prisoner. Dostoevsky would have none of it. He sympathized with reforms of the new tsar, Alexander II, and the pending emancipation of the serfs in 1861, but he distrusted extremes of radicalism, especially its ridiculing of religion. What he really wanted was to start a magazine—a regular source of income if successful and an assured outlet for his own writing. With his brother Mikhail as ostensible owner and business manager (as an ex-convict he could not publicly control the magazine) and Dostoevsky as editor, the first issue of *Time* appeared in 1861. It was an immediate success, not only because of Dostoevsky's editorial skills, but also because *Time*'s announced ideological position—a compromise between contending Slavophiles and Westernizers among the intelligentsia—urged both factions to join with the common people and seek in these children of the soil the national spirit and salvation of the nation. This conviction, which had dawned on Dostoevsky in prison, now proved to be a popular approach, and he introduced various elements of it in his journalistic writings and fiction.

Old and new like-minded friends rallied around Dostoevsky and his magazine, some of whom were to have considerable influence on his political, social, and artistic views, such as the poet Apollon Maikov and the critics Apollon Grigoriev and N. N. Strakhov. They supported his renewed defense of the autonomy of art, a continuation of his old battle with the deceased Belinsky, whose utilitarian view of literature was now more rigidly advocated by the radical-democratic critics N. G. Chernyshevsky and N. A. Dobrolyubov. "Art is always contemporary and real," Dostoevsky argued, but one cannot impose various designs on it because it has "its own integral, organic life."

During these first years of his return to Petersburg Dostoevsky wrote *The House of the Dead*, an amazing performance which regained for him something of the popularity he had enjoyed on the publication of *Poor Folk*. He originally planned it as a novel based on a horrific episode he heard at Omsk, and he jotted down notes for it during stays in the prison hospital. But it ultimately took the form of memoirs of a man condemned

[19]

to ten years for killing his wife. The book is really a faithful record of Dostoevsky's own experiences in prison; part of it first appeared in a newspaper, but then this and the remainder were printed in the 1861–62 issues of *Time*. Turgenev and Herzen acclaimed it, and Tolstoy valued it as Dostoevsky's best work.

He strove for impersonality and objectivity, for he realized that these qualities would contribute artistically to the authenticity of the account. The plan of the work is carefully thought out: first a general description of prison life; then a consideration of social types among the inmates, with deeper psychological studies of the more striking convicts; and finally a kind of history of this form of penal existence illustrated by detailed realistic descriptions of certain episodes, such as the highly diverting Christmas theatricals of the convicts and the wonderful scene of the prisoners' communal bath, a pandemonium that is "simply Dantean," Turgenev declared. However, running through the whole book is the unifying motif of liberty which these convicts had lost. It is effectively symbolized by their unconscious efforts to imitate the behavior of free men, and by the wounded eagle the prisoners had caught and then happily set free. In the acute psychological studies of such unusual convicts as Gazin and Orlov, indomitable criminal types for whom ordinary morality is childish and reason completely subordinated to the unrelenting will to evil, Dostoevsky gained fresh insights that served him well in handling criminal aspects of such creations as Valkovsky, Raskolnikov, Svidrigailov, and Stavrogin. Yet there emerges from the book Dostoevsky's new conviction that among these rough and lowly convicts were many of Russia's most "extraordinary people."

While writing *The House of the Dead* Dostoevsky was also working on his novel *The Insulted and Injured*, which likewise appeared in the pages of *Time* in 1861. It was to be "a novel with an idea," he remarked, "and it will bring me into fashion." Though critics roasted the work, the reading public applauded it. Three years later he rather lamely apologized: since the magazine urgently needed a novel, he had obliged, and hence there were in it "walking texts and not characters"; if "a crude work had emerged," there were "two most serious characters portrayed very faithfully and artistically" and "a half hundred pages of which I am proud."

Readers today would agree and perhaps add that in *The Insulted and Injured* one can detect the authentic feel and atmosphere of the great novels. The idea he mentioned—and novels about ideas were to become a fixed feature of later masterpieces—concerns a woman's right to offer her love to the man of her choice in defiance of convention and family control. The idea is not well sustained; it is lost in the maze of plot and sentimental melodrama inspired by Hoffman, Sue, Hugo, and even Dickens. Vanya loves Natasha but he does everything in his power to aid her love for Alyosha; Alyosha in turn loves both Natasha and Katya, and each girl is eager to further the suit of the other. Then this love in triplicate is confounded by little Nellie's love for Vanya.

It is not difficult to guess that Natasha is one of the "two most serious characters." Though aspects of emotional dualism of women in love had been touched on in Dostoevsky's previous writings, Natasha is the first fully portrayed representative of the type which reappears repeatedly in later novels. Dostoevsky writes of her: "She anticipated with pleasure the happiness of loving endlessly and torturing the man she loved simply because she loved him and that was why perhaps she hastened to give herself to him as a sacrifice."

Nor can there be any doubt that little Nellie is the second character, an absorbing psychological study of a child of thirteen in her initial experience with real love. She is the first of those Dostoevskian females who, as he remarks in the novel, "smothered her own impulses; sympathetic but locked up in pride and inaccessibility."

Vanya, the narrator, qualifies as one of the "walking texts" Dostoevsky mentioned—method of narration was always a major problem in stylistics; Dostoevsky employed, singly or in combination, the omniscient author, confession, diary, memoirs, and notes. Yet Vanya takes on a special interest, for he is a writer and up to a point his career is a faithful transcript of Dostoevsky's before his arrest.

If the novel can be said to have a hero, it is the anti-hero Prince Valkovsky; his wickedness dominates all plot-lines of the work. In unmotivated villainy he is a direct descendant of those fearsome convicts Gazin and Orlov in *The House of the Dead*. But unlike them, he is not instinctively amoral. Dostoevsky even attempts, unconvincingly, to provide motives for his evil-doing. In the defeat of natural goodness by evil, the burden of the novel, the spiritual experience of penal servitude had not yet taught Dostoevsky how to transmute typical villains of melodrama into the artistic criminal types of his masterpieces.

My name is worth a million, Dostoevsky told a friend after his recent popular literary successes. Leaving the magazine and his ailing wife in charge of his brother, he set out, in the summer of 1862, to realize an old dream—a trip to Europe. At the end of ten weeks he was back in Russia after visits to various European capitals, and in the fall of 1863 there appeared in *Time* his essay "Winter Notes on Summer Impressions." His observations only served to strengthen his faith in the future lofty destiny of Russia if it could be kept free from the poison of the West. The evils of bourgeois civilization he saw in Berlin, Paris, and London distressed him, and the socialist remedy advocated was worse.

In 1863 the government suppressed *Time* because of a seemingly unpatriotic article on the Polish rebellion. At this critical juncture Dostoevsky again left for Europe to seek a cure, he said, for his epilepsy. But it is also known that he hoped to repair his precarious finances at gambling resorts abroad and keep a rendezvous with a beautiful St. Petersburg girl, Polina Suslova, with whom he was in love. His luck with both was execrable—he lost at roulette and Polina jilted him. He returned to find his wife dying of tuberculosis and his financial affairs in a desperate state. However, an opportune legacy enabled him to revive the magazine, but only if he altered its name.

Epoch began to appear early in 1864. It got off to a bad start by identifying itself with Dostoevsky's now sharply conservative position. In fact, his first major contribution, *Notes from the Underground*, is in part a satire of the radicals, especially Chernyshevsky. The underground man inveighs against the egoism of socialists who believe that human beings can be governed by rational self-interest.

But this remarkable work is infinitely more than a polemic, for it reveals, among other achievements, a capacity for psychological analysis unique in literature. "I place strong hopes in it," Dostoevsky wrote his brother. "It will be a powerful and frank thing; it will be truth." If one were to separate his total production into two creative periods, the dividing date would be 1864, for *Notes from the Underground* marks a new emphasis in the more or less uniform pattern of his writings up to this point.

Previous heroes lack a deep moral consciousness of their own personalities. They seem incapable of analyzing their thoughts and feelings in relation to the world in which they live. In this respect the hero of *Notes from the Underground* represents an altered approach to characterization. The underground man is a profound analyst of himself and others. He is deeply, morbidly conscious of his personality and an astute logician in explaining its complex nature. The work highlights what had only been suggested earlier—Dostoevsky's searching dialectic, his extraordinary ability to dramatize conflicts of the human mind. And this feature distinguishes the remaining masterpieces.

Notes from the Underground is cast in the form of a "confession," but Dostoevsky adroitly suggests the presence of an unseen interlocutor whose reactions and implied gestures to what the hero says convey to his monologue the heightened impression of overhearing a telephone conversation. When the Soviet scholar M. M. Bakhtin observed that all Dostoevsky's heroes are characterized by their language, he might have added that the verbal portrait of the underground man is the most expressive of them.

In the first part the underground man, an unhappy individual of about forty, engages in a microscopic analysis of himself. It is soon apparent that he is one of those dualistic creatures of the early tales with the important difference that he is fully aware of his dualism. In fact, an irresistible urge to discuss the contradictions of his nature is the entire substance of his self-analysis. He is the supreme alienated man for whom no truth is absolute and every good is relative. His dissection leads him to the conclusion that his ambivalence is based on one fundamental opposition—a conflict between will and reason. For him the whole meaning of human existence lies in self-assertion of the irrational will.

In the second part the underground man relates experiences which illustrate his dualism, and its possible resolution is suggested in the episode with the prostitute who possesses Christian pity and love and therefore can be saved, whereas he has only reason to fall back on and is cut off from life. A more explicit resolution, deleted by the censor, indicated that his salvation was to be found in the realization of a need for faith in Christ.

At the end, however, the struggle between will and reason in the underground man is still unresolved and Dostoevsky left it so in future editions. It is little wonder that Nietzsche's joy was "extraordinary" when he first read the work, in which he discovered "music, very strange, very un-Germanic music." Indeed, on a purely metaphysical level the first part may be regarded as an overture to existentialism. The hero would fit very well into the tragic and absurd condition of life which Sartre allots to man.

Dostoevsky's emphasis, however, is on the spiritual life of dislocated man in a real and acceptable world, and in this sense *Notes from the Underground* is the philosophical introduction to the forthcoming cycle of great novels. Their basic motifs appear in this introduction. Dostoevsky had taken a long step forward in intellectualizing a favorite type character and in involving it with religious, political, and social ideas of immeasurable importance in his later fiction.

In the course of fifteen months (April, 1864–June, 1865) misfortunes overwhelmed Dostoevsky: his wife died, also his brother Mikhail, mainstay of *Epoch*, and finally the magazine expired. Burdened with debts (the magazine's and those of his brother's family which he assumed), he accepted a trifling advance from a shyster bookdealer for a novel, with the stipulation that if the manuscript were not delivered by November 1, 1866, all rights to his published and future writings would belong to this exploiter. To escape a debtor's prison he fled abroad in July, 1865, and repeated the debacle of his second trip to Europe—he lost at gambling the little money he had and endured another frustrated meeting with Polina Suslova.

While in Wiesbaden frantically trying to raise funds to pay hotel bills and return home, Dostoevsky wrote M. N. Katkov, editor of the *Russian Messenger*, to plead for an advance on a novel. The letter contains a rather detailed outline of *Crime and*

[25]

Punishment: "the psychological account of a crime" of an expelled university student sunk in utter poverty. "Under the influence of strange, 'incomplete' ideas which go floating about" he decides to kill and rob a useless old woman, a moneylender, save his poor mother and sister, then finish his education and expiate his crime by good deeds. After the murder, "insoluble questions confront" him. He feels "cut off from mankind" and confesses because "*he himself experiences a moral need*" for punishment. Katkov sent the advance and Dostoevsky went back to Russia to write the novel. It was published in the *Russian Messenger* during 1866 and aroused great popular interest.

Actually, Dostoevsky had conceived *Crime and Punishment* years before—he thought of it then as the confession of a convict. And before he left for Europe in 1865 he had vainly sought an advance for still another story he was writing, "The Drunkards," which, he told the editor, would concern not only the question of drunkenness but "all its ramifications, especially the picture of a family and the rearing of children in these circumstances." Clearly this had to do with the remarkable character Marmeladov and his equally remarkable family which Dostoevsky now worked into the design of *Crime and Punishment*.

The tremendous effort he expended on the work is revealed in Dostoevsky's notebooks (notebooks for his last five novels have been published in Russia). They take us into his laboratory, as it were, and these rough drafts, preliminary sketches of characters and scenes, and above all his corrections and observations, extending to the minutest details of the material, provide a deep insight into the creative process of a literary genius and the infinite pains he took with everything that made for artistic perfection.

Crime and Punishment is closely involved with contemporary events. Dostoevsky's own poverty at the time and the financial crisis in Russia in the 1860s provide background for Raskolnikov's situation and exacerbated state of mind. Money is at the root of his difficulties and in one way or another determines the thoughts and actions also of the Marmeladovs, Sonya, Luzhin, Lebezyatnikov, and Svidrigailov. Raskolnikov's theory of the right to kill on the premise that a noble end justifies illicit means was no doubt suggested by Rastignac's theorizing in Balzac's *Père Goriot*. This proposition, an outgrowth of the "incomplete ideas" of the time mentioned by Dostoevsky, amounts to a continuation of his attacks on the materialist philosophy of the radicals. The hero is one of them, a profoundly human, suffering nihilist, in whose soul life and theory conflict. On one level, in fact, the work is a social novel, a satirical debunking of radical youth preaching Chernyshevsky's doctrine of revolutionary democracy.

But the novel's focus concerns Raskolnikov's tormented struggle between good and evil. Dostoevsky goes well beyond the "idea of Rastignac" in dissecting the impulses that lead his dualistic hero to kill and then to repent. In these respects the complex motivation is absorbingly reflected in conflicting trial flights in the notebooks. At one point in the notes Dostoevsky warns himself: "The main anatomy of the novel: it is of crucial importance to bring the matter to a real climax and do away with this vagueness, that is, *explain the murder in one manner or another* and establish his character and attitudes clearly." Although motivation for the murder is ambiguous, the novel's central idea is unmistakable: reason cannot take the place of the living process of life. For Raskolnikov, dialectics had taken the place of life. In prison his satanic pride, which had led him to violate the moral law, gives way to the realization that happiness cannot be achieved by a reasoned plan of existence but must be earned by suffering.

[27]

Though Raskolnikov dominates the novel, in none of Dostoevsky's previous fiction had the secondary characters been so well individualized, especially the Marmeladov family, and the meek, ineffable Sonya, who is the hero's good angel as the mysterious Svidrigailov is his evil angel. In these and others, all reality, as in the case of Raskolnikov, becomes an element in their self-knowledge. Dostoevsky had given entirely new dimensions to the detective story by brilliantly infusing into it compelling philosophical, psychological, and social elements. The unity and concentration of the action, with each episode advancing the development of the central theme, and all of this cast against a background of vividly described Petersburg life that adds meaning and tone to the behavior of the characters, made *Crime and Punishment*, compositionally speaking, the best of Dostoevsky's materpieces.

As sheer story, however, the novel does not rest on dialectics, morality, or the central idea, although these features contribute to its total impression. It is the high seriousness of this drama of crime that attracts the reader. The intensity of the step-by-step revelation of Raskolnikov's plan, the thrilling account of the murder, and then the equally intense psychological analysis of the disintegration of all the forces that had goaded him on to kill—this is the vital story that never loses its grip on the reader's imagination and emotions. And over all radiates a spiritual glow that illumines the darkest recesses of the criminal, of the morally debased and inspires them to seek a deeper meaning in life through suffering to ultimate salvation.

While working on the last part of *Crime and Punishment*, Dostoevsky remembered his contract with the bookseller to deliver the manscript of a novel. The date was fast approaching and postponement was denied. Fortunately three years before he had outlined a novel about a rebel against society who abandons Russia for Europe to devote himself entirely to gambling. He now took up this subject, hired a young stenographer, Anna Snitkina, and in twenty-six days dictated a short novel, *The Gambler* (1866). The work is plainly based on his own passion for gambling and his equally passionate love affair with Polina Suslova. The story centers on the love-hate relationship of Polina Alexandrovna, an imperious beauty, and the gambler Alexei Ivanovich. This masochistic-sadistic emotional duel is an intensified and exaggerated reflection of the relations of Dostoevsky and Polina Suslova. Created in such haste, *The Gambler* was bound to be a minor effort, but it has several powerful scenes that develop further the psychological manifestations of the love-hate syndrome that dominates the relations of a number of Dostoevsky's men and women.

The stenographer, who was twenty-five years younger than Dostoevsky, soon married him (February, 1867). She resented his in-laws' continued demands on his meager funds and wisely suggested going abroad when creditors once more threatened prosecution. They remained in Europe four years, traveling from country to country. Anna endured long periods of abject poverty when Dostoevsky lost previous advances and money from everything he could pawn in his craze for gambling. There were also epileptic fits, a revival of his love for Polina Suslova, the tragic death of their firstborn, and attacks of sick, nervous irritability. But her devotion to him and his genius never faltered. Dostoevsky's second marriage was one of real love and the most fortunate event in his life.

Abroad he tried to keep informed of happenings in Russia and Europe by avidly reading newspapers and magazines, and by correspondence with literary friends at home. At Geneva he attended meetings of the International League for Peace and Freedom where clarion calls to bloody revolution by fiery orators such as Bakunin and diatribes against Christianity horrified him. He worried over their influence on like-minded people in Russia, and it was in this disturbed state that he began, in 1867, to think about his next work.

Of all Dostoevsky's novels, *The Idiot* was the most difficult to write. The starting point is a court trial he read in the Russian press about gentry parents who had tortured their children, particularly a daughter of fifteen. He not infrequently drew upon newspaper accounts of domestic tragedies and criminal cases for his fiction, and he defended the practice because of the quality it imparted to his conception of realism. "I have my own special view of reality in art," he wrote a correspondent. "What the majority call almost fantastic and exceptional sometimes signifies for me the very essence of reality. . . . In every issue of a newspaper you meet accounts of the most real facts and amazing happenings. For our writers they are fantastic; they are not concerned with them; yet they are reality because they are facts."

Here Dostoevsky has in mind his great rivals Turgenev and Tolstoy, whose depictions of the gentry class, he believed, dealt with typical, surface features of reality. "I have an understanding of reality and realism entirely different from that of our realists and critics," he wrote another correspondent. "My idealism is more real than theirs. Lord! To relate sensibly all that we Russians have experienced in our last ten years of spiritual growth—indeed, do not our realists cry out that this is fantasy! Nevertheless, this is primordial, real realism!" In one of his finest short stories, "A Gentle Creature" (1876), we observe him in the process of transmuting "the fantastic facts of reality" into art—a brief press release of a young wife who jumped to her death with an ikon clasped to her breast is passed through the alembic of his analytical mind as he imagines a frame of action consistent with psychological realism and the truth of the tragedy.

But Dostoevsky added an important dimension to his notion of "fantastic realism." He preferred to shift the emphasis from the external world to that of the mind and heart of his characters, for he was primarily interested in the realities of their spiritual existence. Art he regarded as a medium for conveying the wisdom of life, the emotions of the soul. Though convinced that he was fundamentally concerned with social, intellectual, and spiritual problems of average Russians, he insisted that he elevated them to universal significance in his search—as he put it—"with complete realism to find man in man." He defined his innovation as an attempt to represent in fiction spiritual phenomena above and beyond social practices, to resolve the psychological contradictions of man in terms of true and eternal "humanness." "They call me a psychologist," he wrote in his notebook. "It is not true. I'm only a realist in the higher sense; that is, I portray all the depths of the human soul."

A study of the copious notebook material of *The Idiot* shows how the "fantastic realism" of the newspaper report of the trial was eventually transformed into what can only be described as a form of "mystical realism." In the notes Dostoevsky piles up plan after plan, at least eight of them, in an effort to grasp clearly the novel's plot and characters. Family groups appear and disappear, heroes and heroines shove each other off the front stage, lineaments of one possible protagonist are transferred to another, and incidents of murder, suicide, rape, theft, and arson compete for attention. In the early plans the principal character is a typical Dostoevskian Double with traits utterly unlike those of the finished novel's meek hero.

In this bewildering mélange of plot, counterplot, and unresolved characters, what obviously frustrated Dostoevsky was inability to hit upon a central idea and a hero who fully embodied it. Not until the sixth plan does he suddenly formulate the idea and the image of the character to represent it—

[31]

the idiot, Prince Myshkin. "The chief idea of the novel," he wrote his niece at this point, "is to portray the positively beautiful man [in a moral sense]. . . . The good is an ideal, but the ideal, both ours and that of civilized Europe, is still far from having been worked out. There is only one positively beautiful man in the world—Christ." But Dostoevsky pulls away from this abyss, for in the novel the "divine character" of Myshkin vanishes as the radiance of his pure moral nature is stained by human weaknesses. However, there is nothing humorous in Myshkin, as some critics have maintained. "If Don Quixote and Pickwick as philanthropists are charming," Dostoevsky jotted down in his notes, "it is because they are comical. The hero of this novel, the Prince, is not comical but does have another charming quality—he is *innocent!*"

In the fantastic world of the Epanchins, Ivolgins, and their hangers-on, the main action concerns the love affairs of Rogozhin, Ganya, Nastasya, and Aglaya. From the ensuing complications emerge most of the superb scenes. But Dostoevsky carefully avoids emphasizing Myshkin's spirituality solely in relation to these love intrigues by providing a field of action for him. It is described as the "dark forces" of the new generation given to sensuality, the accumulation of wealth, and even to crime. All characters are drawn into this crisis of moral decline, and Myshkin alone stands opposed to the "dark forces," preaching his ineffectual doctrine of service, compassion, brotherly love, and man's salvation through the image of Christ. He tells all that the world is beautiful and life is happiness. Despite his faith, he fails. Nearly everyone looks down upon him and his experiences are symbolic of Christ's among the Pharisees. In the end the sinning people he comes in contact with or influences are rendered unhappy and he himself lapses into idiocy.

The story of Myshkin has sometimes been regarded as Dostoevsky's own spiritual biography. But the image of the "positively beautiful" hero does not wholly succeed. Dostoevsky himself seems to have had misgivings on this score, for he wrote Strakhov: "In the novel much was composed in haste, much is prolix and has not succeeded. I do not stand behind the novel. I stand behind my idea." Nevertheless, he had written one of the great novels of world literature.

In attempting to create a morally perfect hero, Dostoevsky had gambled with popular interest. Readers were baffled by *The Idiot* and critics regarded it as a falling off after the tremendously successful *Crime and Punishment*. Further, publishers were not eager to buy up the book rights, and long before the last installment appeared (February, 1869), Dostoevsky was in Katkov's debt for another novel. Expenses attendant upon the birth of his second child at this time took every available penny and he eagerly accepted a small advance from Strakhov for a short story which turned into a short novel, *The Eternal Husband* (1870). Its smooth narrative style and well-constructed plot about a husband, Pavel Pavlovich, born to be cuckolded—in this case by his friend Velchaninov—contribute to a singularly fine achievement in fiction form. The tale seems like a deliberate exercise piece in Dostoevsky's now finished psychological technique; concentration is mostly on analysis, whereas characters and scenes echo those in previous works. In the careful dissection of Pavel Pavlovich's ambivalent thoughts and actions after he has discovered his friend's betrayal of him, one is reminded of how much Dostoevsky's writing is identified with the history of the human consciousness in its tragic duality.

Meanwhile Dostoevsky had been contemplating a large novel, entitled "Atheism," about a Russian who loses his faith in God and through experiences with people of various intellectual, philosophical, and religious persuasions falls into a state of complete self-abasement. Finally, he rediscovers a stronger faith in the Russian Christ and the Russian soil.

Some months later this project merged into a still vaster one designed as five separate but connected novels to be called "The Life of a Great Sinner." The extant notes indicate that Dostoevsky intended to portray his hero from childhood to manhood. He is involved in numerous adventures, including a blasphemous crime that compels a stay in a monastery. Having rejected God, he wanders over Russia, indulges in debauchery, and encounters real figures of a past epoch of vigorous Orthodoxy and well-known representatives among Slavophiles and Westernizers. Christ and anti-Christ, Russia and Europe are debated and the battlefield of this Dostoevskian conflict is the hearts of men and women of the novel. In the end the hero achieves sincere love, confesses his sins, and establishes a new life in faith in God and in pious good deeds. To portray a great sinner's spiritual pilgrimage through an evil world of little faith to the distant goal of salvation, which he gains through suffering and glorifies by saintliness, was the end of Dostoevsky's creative scheme of things. "This novel is my entire hope," he wrote his niece, "and the whole expectation of my life."

Although "The Life of a Great Sinner" was to remain just another of Dostoevsky's unwritten novels, it cast its shadow over nearly everything else he did write, and he pilfered scenes, incidents, and characters from its outline to piece out the imperfections of what he considered lesser works. This is true of his next novel, *The Devils* (better known in English as *The Possessed*), which he began at the end of 1869, putting aside his projected *magnum opus* in order to send Katkov a work long since promised. For subject he once again seized upon a "fantastic" event in the press—members of a Moscow student revolutionary cell, headed by S. G. Nechaev, a disciple of Bakunin, murdered a comrade who, they suspected, intended to betray them. Initially Dostoevsky thought of it as a short "pamphlet-novel," a frankly tendentious fictionized treatment of the murder which would give him an opportunity to speak out more directly against radicals who, he believed, were threatening to undermine Russia. But the work soon took on the proportions of a full-length novel and is one of his indubitable masterpieces. As in the case of *The Idiot,* notebooks for *The Possessed* provide valuable information on the labor he expended in formulating his central idea and the hero who would embody it, in defining numerous other characters in a story packed with action and drama, and in working out the intricacies of an involved plot. Various complications resulted from efforts to regard the young radicals of the newspaper accounts as direct descendants of idealistic revolutionaries of his own generation of the 1840s. The notes indicate that several characters are based upon real figures he knew; others are composites of people in his own life.

After almost a year of work, he destroyed much of what he had written, for facts of living reality served only to inspire his imagination. Features and figures in the plan of "The Life of a Great Sinner" had begun to fuse in his mind with the Nechaev affair. For the initial hero, Pyotr Verkhovensky (Nechaev), he substituted Stavrogin, suggested by the unnamed hero of "The Life of a Great Sinner," and the novel's field of action was extended to involve, besides revolutionary conspiracy, some of those profound questions of religion and morality implicit in the design of his unwritten *magnum opus.* He had finally hit upon his central idea. He wrote Maikov that the malady afflicting youth in the 1840s had not ended; the devils had gone out of the Russians and entered into a herd of swine, into the Nechaevs, had drowned, and the healed man, from whom the devils had gone out, was seated at the feet of Jesus. "The whole

[35]

vocation of Russia," Dostoevsky continued, "is contained in Orthdoxy, in the *light from the East*, which will stream to mankind blinded in the West because it has lost Christ. . . . Well, if you want to know, this is precisely the theme of my novel. It is called 'The Devils'!"

The Possessed's first chapters appeared in Katkov's *Russian Messenger* in January, 1871. At this point Dostoevsky faltered. He was ill, out of funds again, and had become convinced that he could complete the novel only in Russia. Katkov sent him the fare and Dostoevsky returned to Petersburg in July in time to attend the trial of Nechaev and his co-conspirators. His enthusiasm for the novel revived, and by the end of 1872 the last parts were published.

Stavrogin, who dominates the work, was intended by Dostoevsky to integrate its two thematic divisions, the romantic element suggested in part by the plan for "The Life of a Great Sinner," and the revolutionary conspiracy inspired by the Nechaev affair. In Stavrogin, Dostoevsky underlines in his notes, *"is the whole pathos of the novel . . . he is the hero."* His personal magnetism draws all to him, and he exerts a powerful influence, especially on Pyotr Verkhovensky, Shatov, and Kirilov. If we may judge from notebooks and novel, however, Dostoevsky never freed himself from a degree of uncertainty about Stavrogin's image. The ambiguities of his spiritual and political contacts with various conspirators are matched by those reflected in his relations with the principal women: Liza, Darya, and crippled Marya Timofeevna whom he marries to make a martyr of himself and also to outrage people's feelings. Though this obscurity has convinced some critics that Dostoevsky wished to convey a profound symbolic truth in Stavrogin, the notebooks reveal that he deliberately made him mysterious, which may be a tacit admission of artistic defeat in portraying a character that originally had so much potential significance for him. But the function Stavrogin ultimately fulfills is skillfully maintained and highly effective. In his inner struggle he reaches a stage of psychological amoralism in which he is unable to distinguish between good and evil. "At Tiknon," the famous chapter concerning Stavrogin's violation of the little girl, which Katkov refused to print, is of primary importance for an understanding of the characterization. There it becomes plain that the forces of evil have taken full possession of Stavrogin; he has lost faith in God and as a consequence the innate goodness of his nature has utterly atrophied. Only one way out remains—suicide.

The reformed radical Shatov and not Stavrogin is the principal bearer of ideas which amount to Dostoevsky's ideological answer to the would-be revolutionists. Their amazing meeting is a travesty of the movement, and their leader, Pytor Verkhovensky, is a half-comic, melodramatic villain. The other conspirators, Virginsky, Shigalev, *et al.*, are described as dolts, eccentrics, and rascals who lack their leader's courage. In his treatment of the revolutionists and their activities, Dostoevsky's powerful dialectical method is sacrificed to a polemical purpose.

The old liberal, Stepan Trofimovich Verkhovensky, father of the bloodthirsty Pyotr, is brilliantly depicted as a kind of Russian Don Quixote, in whose image Dostoevsky pokes fun at the political and social beliefs of his own youth. When this lovable old man is off stage, interest in the narrative noticeably wanes. At the novel's conclusion the last vestige of Stepan's liberalism vanishes before the new faith he has acquired in the religion of the common people whom he had formerly scorned.

The Possessed revived Dostoevsky's popularity, which was further enhanced, after his return from Europe, by impressive public readings from his works. He now began to frequent conservative social gatherings where he made friends with prominent people, some of whom were close to the throne, such as the powerful Senator K. P. Pobedonostsev. Such connections helped to secure Dostoevsky's appointment as editor of the conservative weekly, *The Citizen*, in January, 1873. But its reactionary emphasis proved even too much for him and he resigned, after a little more than a year, in April, 1874. Fortunately his financial condition had improved, for his wife had undertaken the publication of his works from which a substantial income was obtained.

During his editorship of *The Citizen*, Dostoevsky contributed to it a column, *The Diary of a Writer*, and after his resignation he revived it, in January, 1876, as a separate monthly publication. He continued it for more than a year and also published additional numbers in 1880 and 1881. *The Diary* contains reporting on current events, such as court trials, suicides, spiritualism, conditions of children working in factories, but he also used it as a medium for expressing ideas on broad social, political, and religious questions. In its pages may also be found literary reminiscences and criticism, autobiographical matter, and short stories and sketches: "Vlas," "Bobok," "The Peasant Marei," "The Heavenly Christmas Tree," "A Gentle Creature," and "The Dream of a Ridiculous Man," which contains Dostoevsky's best presentation of "The Golden Age"—a vision of earth before the fall—that captivates several of his heroes. Behind *The Diary*, however, is a larger purpose. Journalism and literature were closely allied in his mind, for he firmly believed that the interrelation of art and reality must center in the observation of daily existence, and he draws upon such material in this publication for his fiction. *The Diary* attracted numerous readers and is of major importance in any study of Dostoevsky's views as well as his remaining novels.

In *The Diary* Dostoevsky tells of the origin of his next novel, *A Raw Youth* (1875): the confession of the illegitimate, unfledged Arkady Dolgoruky about his adventures in the social world of Petersburg where he seeks his father whom he hates for neglecting him so long but whose parental affection he yearns for. There is an appealing freshness in Dolgoruky who is portrayed with keen awareness of the thoughts, confusion, bravado, sensitiveness, and idealism of youth. In the characterization, as well as in much else connected with the work, Dostoevsky once again borrows from his plan for the unwritten "Life of a Great Sinner."

When Dolgoruky finally discovers his father, Versilov, interest shifts and he virtually supplants the son as hero. There is some truth in the observation that Dostoevsky despairingly made to his wife: "there are four novels in *A Raw Youth*." For at the end of the first part, he all but strangles the plot in excessive motivation forced upon him by introducing a profusion of new characters. Besides the initial theme, three others are developed, and a fifth barely adumbrated. The ensuing intrigue involves several love stories, the struggle between father and son for possession of the beautiful Katerina Akhmakova, and a mysterious letter compromising her, sewed in the lining of Dolgoruky's clothes, which all the chief characters desperately strive to obtain for their own nefarious purposes. The incomplete fifth theme, only tenuously connected with the novel, concerns a group of revolutionary conspirators, again based upon a newspaper account of their activities. On this occasion the surprising fact is that Dostoevsky portrays the radicals almost as heroes, at least compared with the "devils" in *The Possessed*.

Versilov is the most fascinating character and his puzzling personality recalls that of the enigmatic Stavrogin. He is developed in much the same manner—by flashbacks, hearsay, and the effect he has on other people. Like Stavrogin, the final portrait leaves an incomplete but powerful impression. As a

[39]

Russian nobleman Versilov is cynical in matters political, believes that no class is so fond of idleness as the toiling masses, and maintains that the delights of labor have been invented by the idle from virtuous motives. His attachment to God is purely sentimental, but he tells his son that the idea of virtue without Christ is the idea of all modern civilization—a Dostoevskian conviction. He also echoes Dostoevsky's favorite belief that Europe stands on the brink of destruction because of her revolutionary materialism and denial of Christ, that Russia, which lives not for itself but for the whole world, will in the end lead Europe to the kingdom of God and salvation.

In connection with the ambivalent Versilov, Dostoevsky for the first time is emphatically explicit about the underlying principles that inspired his preoccupation with dualism in the portrayal of some of his greatest characters. Its psychological manifestation as the determinant of thought, feeling, and action is demonstrably a reflection of the part that dualism played in his own nature.

A Raw Youth is usually ranked beneath the other great novels of Dostoevsky's last period. The notebooks, which have only recently been published in full in the Soviet Union and are more nearly complete than those for any of his novels, indicate that his intentions were unrealized in the finished work. For one thing, the notes call for an expansive attack on contemporary social evils which is lacking in *A Raw Youth*. He seems somehow to have got lost in the complexity of plot. The Dostoevskian quality of inwardness is noticeably absent, and the customary concern of his characters with profound moral and religious problems, while occasionally evident on the surface, never penetrates to the core of their relation to life. Action does not develop into thought but often becomes an end in itself. This failure no doubt arises from lack of a convincing central idea which in the masterpieces provides the dynamics of thought and contributes so much to artistic integration of the total work. Dostoevsky explained that the first stage of his creative process was that of the "poet"—an effort of imaginative inspiration that resulted in the formulation of the central idea of a novel. The next stage he described as "the activity of the artist"—concretizing from his drafts and notes the finished work itself. The notebooks for *A Raw Youth* indicate that to a considerable extent he had been less than successful in both stages.

In the last issue of *The Diary of a Writer* for December, 1877, Dostoevsky tells his readers that he is discontinuing it in order to devote himself to an artistic work that had been "imperceptibly and involuntarily composing itself" in his mind during the past two years. *The Brothers Karamazov* began to appear in the *Russian Messenger* in January, 1879, and the last chapter was completed in November, 1880.

In a sense Dostoevsky had been preparing for this supreme effort throughout most of his creative life. The major theme—the charge of parricide against the innocent Dmitri and the judicial error that resulted in his conviction—was based on a convict's account that Dostoevsky had heard in his Siberian prison. The section on the boys' club, involving Kolya Krasotkin and little Ilyusha, derives from a discarded episode in notes for *The Idiot*. *The Diary of a Writer* contains much material that has a direct bearing on the subject matter and ideas of the novel. The plan of "The Life of a Great Sinner" contributes its increment, especially in the characterizations of Alyosha and Zosima. And several character-types, which he had been developing since he began to write fiction, achieve their fullest expression in this last work.

Although *The Brothers Karamazov* is Dostoevsky's longest novel, the plot's bare outline may be summarized in a few sentences: the story of a crime in which Dmitri Karamazov and his father are rivals for Grushenka's love. Prompted by the second son Ivan, an illegitimate son Smerdyakov murders the father and Dmitri is accused and convicted on circumstantial evidence.

But into this sordid tale Dostoevsky introduces a titanic struggle of love and hate with all its psychological and spiritual implications, cast against a background of the life of a town and monastery. Throughout the whole work there persists a search for faith, for God—the central idea of the novel. In no other masterpiece has the white-hot intensity of his ideological world glowed so brightly or has he spiritualized ideas so arrestingly and profoundly. In it are concentrated all his mature art, wisdom, and doubts. All that life meant for him—its experiences, symbols, and vision—is reflected in these extraordinary characters.

Although nothing in human experience may satisfactorily explain the extreme motives and actions of old Karamazov, his sons, Zosima, Grushenka, and Katerina Ivanovna, nevertheless these characters, like symbols or personifications of ideas in a modern allegory of life, are treated so realistically that we effect a willing suspension of disbelief and accept them as living human beings. In such creations artistic reality tends to approximate spiritual reality or ideas of spiritual reality.

The father has left his mark on each son. This Karamazov taint is carnal sensuality which, in its less vicious manifestations, Dostoevsky describes as "a zest for life." It is the father's dominating trait, ruins Dmitri, is just below the surface in Ivan, and even rears its ugly head in the saintlike Alyosha. All the Karamazovs are philosophers, Dmitri remarks, and the animal instinct in them constantly struggles with the moral and spiritual side of their natures.

Alyosha, as the notes indicate, took shape earliest in Dostoevsky's mind, and his description in the novel as "the future hero of my story" suggests that the author hoped to continue his development in one or more sequels. Alyosha was destined to undergo the hero's holy pilgrimage in the plan of "The Life of a Great Sinner." The only brother who loves life more than the meaning of life, Alyosha is identified with the Christian ideal. Though in the sequel Dostoevsky obviously intended him to sin in making his way through the purgatory of modern life, he carries in his heart the secret of renewal that will enable him to wrestle with the devil without losing his soul.

Dmitri loves life but its meaning continually puzzles him. Simplicity and deep feeling are the essence of his being. "To hell with all who pry into the human heart!" he exclaims. What troubles him most is that a man of lofty mind begins with the ideal of the Madonna and ends with the ideal of Sodom. Out of a feeling of moral guilt for his father's murder—he had wished for his death—he accepts his conviction. "I want to suffer," he declares, "and by suffering I shall purify myself."

Ivan, who is more concerned with life's meaning than with life itself, is the most absorbing character and in many respects the mental image of his creator. He is the last of Dostoevsky's remarkable series of Doubles and his ambivalence is centered in a cosmic struggle of man with God. Ivan begins with an act of rebellion and ends in utter metaphysical insurrection against God's world. The Karamazov taint in him takes the form of intellectual pride. In his pride he dreams of becoming a man-god, but when the submissive side of his nature predominates, he accepts the world-god, for he cannot understand the higher harmony between man and the world of God. In this inner struggle Ivan is concerned really with those factors which were at the bottom of Dostoevsky's own search for faith—the problem of sin and suffering and their relation to the existence of God.

The resolution of Ivan's struggle is concentrated in the section "Pro and Contra," one of Dostoevsky's finest artistic

[43]

achievements. After recounting to Alyosha the true stories of tortured children, Ivan demands justice for these sins, and not justice in heaven or hell but on earth. If eternal harmony is to be obtained at the expense of these persecuted innocent children, he declares, then he must renounce the harmony of God's world. And when Alyosha insists that Christ, who suffered for the sake of all mankind, had the right to forgive this suffering of the innocent, Ivan counters with the famous "Legend of the Grand Inquisitor," in which the Inquisitor condemns Christ for preaching man's freedom of choice in the knowledge of good and evil. In both the notes and a letter to the novel's editor, Dostoevsky asserts that Ivan's argument rejecting the meaning of God's world is unanswerable and that Ivan also approves the Inquisitor's reason for denying Christ.

In the next section, however, Dostoevsky attempts an answer which he puts in the mouth of the old monk Zosima. It had already appeared in Dostoevsky's own words in *The Diary of a Writer:* that equality is to be found only in the spiritual dignity of man; that suffering does not destroy the harmony of life but is a fulfillment, an act of Godly justice which corrects transgressions for the sake of the whole; that the secret of universal harmony is not achieved by the mind but by the heart, by feeling and faith; that if one loves all living things, this love will justify suffering, all will share in each other's guilt, and suffering for the sins of others will then become the moral duty of every true Christian. This inconclusive debate between Ivan and Zosima reflects the anguished dialogue that went on in Dostoevsky's doubting, dualistic mind in his own search for faith.

Perhaps Dostoevsky intended to elaborate on the answer in the sequel to the novel, but after his celebrated speech at the unveiling of Pushkin's statue, which electrified a distinguished audience with its ringing prophecy of Russia's world mission, he had only a few more months to live. He died January 28,

1881, and with him died the continuation of his great work. More so than any of his other novels, *The Brothers Karamazov* faithfully mirrored the inner struggle that was the source of his art—his mind was with the reasoning of Ivan, his heart with the precepts of Zosima. This mighty conflict of mind and heart adds an element to the novel that transcends mortal experience. There is a sense of infinity in the book which reaches out beyond the earthy passions of its story to a region where exist the ultimate, universalized reasons for all human behavior. It somehow seems to justify Dostoevsky's belief that the higher realism which he took as his province was like that of Shakespeare—not restricted to mere imitations of life but concerned with the mystery of man and the human soul.

SELECTED BIBLIOGRAPHY

NOTE: *The only attempt to publish an edition of the collected works of Dostoevsky's fiction in English translation is* The Novels of Fyodor Dostoevsky, *translated by Constance Garnett (12 vols.; New York, Macmillan, 1921–31).*

The most complete Russian edition of Dostoevsky's letters is Pisma, *Vols. I–IV, edited by A. S. Dolinin (Moscow-Leningrad, 1928–59). A number of letters have ben translated into English in various volumes, but an English version of this four-volume Russian edition is being prepared for publication.*

An extensive amount of journalistic writings in English translation may be found in the following: Dostoevsky's Occasional Writings, *selected, translated, and introduced by David Magarshack (New York, Random House, 1963);* Dostoevsky: The Diary of a Writer, *Vols. I–II, translated and annotated by Boris Brasol (New York, Scribner's, 1949).*

The valuable notebooks for all five of Dostoevsky's major novels have appeared in separate publications in the Soviet Union. English translations of them are now under way. So far three have appeared: The Notebooks for Crime and Punishment, *edited and translated by Edward Wasiolek (Chicago, University of Chicago Press, 1967);* The Notebooks for The Idiot, *edited by Edward Wasiolek, translated by Katharine Strelsky (Chicago, University of Chicago Press, 1967);* The Notebooks for The Possessed, *edited and with an Introduction by Edward Wasiolek, translated by Victor Terras (Chicago, University of Chicago Press, 1968).*

CRITICAL WORKS AND COMMENTARY

NOTE: *Material under this heading is so voluminous, especially if periodical literature is included, that it will be necessary to confine it to a listing of books in English that appear to make important contributions to the subject.*

Belknap, R. L. The Structure of *The Brothers Karamazov.* The Hague, Mouton, 1967.

Berdyaev, Nicholas. Dostoevsky. Tr. Donald Atwater. New York, Meridian Books, 1957.

Camus, Albert. The Rebel: An Essay on Man in Revolt. Tr. Anthony Bower. New York, Knopf, 1954.

Carr, Edward Hallett. Dostoevsky, 1821–1881. London, Allen and Unwin, 1949.

Coulson, Jessie. Dostoevsky: A Self-Portrait. London, Oxford, 1962.

Curle, Richard. Characters of Dostoevsky: Studies from Four Novels. London, Heinemann, 1950.

Fanger, Donald. Dostoevsky and Romantic Realism. Cambridge, Mass., Harvard University Press, 1965.

Gide, André. Dostoevsky. Tr. with an Introduction by Arnold Bennett. New York, Knopf, 1926.

Ivanov, Vyacheslav. Freedom and the Tragic Life: A Study in Dostoevsky. Tr. Norman Cameron. New York, Noonday, 1957.

Jackson, Robert Louis. Dostoevsky's Quest for Form: A Study of His Philosophy of Art. New Haven, Yale University Press, 1966.

Lavrin, Janko. Dostoevsky: A Study. New York, Macmillan, 1947.

Linnér, Sven. Dostoevskij on Realism. Stockholm, Alniquist and Wiksell, 1967.

Matlaw, R. E. The Brothers Karamazov: Novelistic Technique. The Hague, Mouton, 1957.

Meier-Graefe, Julius. Dostoevsky: The Man and His Work. Tr. Herbert H. Marks. New York, Harcourt, 1928.

Merezhkovsky, D. S. Tolstoi as Man and Artist, with an Essay on Dostoevski. New York, Putnam, 1902.

Mochulsky, Konstantin. Dostoevsky: His Life and Works. Tr. Michael A. Minihan. Princeton, Princeton University Press, 1967.

Murry, John Middleton. Fyodor Dostoevsky: A Critical Study. London, Martin Secker, 1923.

Passage, Charles E. Dostoevsky the Adapter: A Study in Dostoevsky's Use of the Tales of Hoffmann. University of North Carolina Studies in Comparative Literature, No. 10. Chapel Hill, University of North Carolina Press, 1954.

Payne, Robert. Dostoevsky: A Human Portrait. New York, Knopf, 1961.

Powys, John Cowper. Dostoevsky: A Study. London, Lane, 1946.

Reeve, F. D. The Russian Novel. New York, McGraw-Hill, 1966.

Roe, Ivan. The Breath of Corruption: An Interpretation of Dostoevsky. London, Hutchinson, 1946.

Simmons, Ernest J. Dostoevski: The Making of a Novelist. New York, Oxford, 1940.

Steiner, George. Tolstoy or Dostoevsky: An Essay in the Old Criticism. New York, Knopf, 1956.

Troyat, Henri. Firebrand: The Life of Dostoevsky. Tr. Norbert Guterman. New York, Roy, 1946.

Wasiolek, Edward. Dostoevsky: The Major Fiction. Cambridge, Mass., M.I.T. Press, 1964.

Yarmolinsky, Avrahm. Dostoevsky: His Life and Art. New York, Criterion Books, 1957.